Community Helpers

Mail Carriers

by Dee Ready

Content Consultant:
Dave Oberle, Supervisor of Customer Service
United States Postal Service

Bridgestone Books
an imprint of Capstone Press

Bridgestone Books are published by Capstone Press
818 North Willow Street, Mankato, Minnesota 56001
http://www.capstone-press.com

Library of Congress Cataloging-in-Publication Data
Ready, Dee.
    Mail carriers/by Dee Ready.
    p. cm.--(Community helpers)
    Includes bibliographical references and index.
    Summary: Explains the clothing, tools, schooling, and work of mail carriers.
    ISBN 1-56065-557-7
    1. Postal service--Letter carriers--Juvenile literature. [1.Postal service--Letter carriers.
    2. Occupations.] I. Title. II. Series: Community helpers (Mankato, Minn.)
HE6161.R43   1998
383'.145'0973--dc21

                       97-2954
                       CIP
                       AC

Editorial credits
Editor, Timothy Larson; Cover design, Timothy Halldin
Photo research assistant, Michelle Norstad

Photo credits
International Stock/Bill Stanton, 16
Maguire PhotoGraFX, 6, 10, 14, 18
Frank W. Mantlik, 20
Unicorn Stock/Joe Sohm, cover, 4; Joel Dexter, 8; Aneal Vohra, 12

Table of Contents

Mail Carriers

Mail carriers make sure that mail goes to the right people. Mail carriers also gather the mail that people send.

What Mail Carriers Do

Mail carriers pick up mail at the post office. A post office is a building where mail is sorted. Then mail carriers walk or drive their routes. A route is the places a mail carrier must go to bring the mail.

What Mail Carriers Wear

Mail carriers wear blue uniforms. In the winter, they wear warm uniforms. They also wear warm shoes and hats. In the summer, many wear shorts and white hats. The shorts and white hats help keep them cool.

Tools Mail Carriers Use

Many mail carriers carry a mail pouch. A pouch is a bag with a flap over the top. A mail pouch can hold up to 35 pounds (16 kilograms) of mail. Other mail carriers carry mail in long plastic trays.

What Mail Carriers Drive

City mail carriers drive white trucks. Country mail carriers drive cars. Mail cars and trucks have steering wheels on the right side. This makes it easier for mail carriers to reach some mailboxes. Everyday cars and trucks have steering wheels on the left side.

Mail Carriers and School

All new mail carriers finish high school. They also pass a postal test. Then other mail carriers teach them about their routes.

Where Mail Carriers Work

Mail carriers take mail to people in towns and in cities. They carry mail to people in the country. Mail carriers bring mail to both people's homes and work places.

People Who Help Mail Carriers

Mail clerks help mail carriers sort mail. Some clerks also sell stamps for letters. Other people help ship mail to post offices. They drive trucks or fly planes.

Mail Carriers Help Others

Mail carriers help communities. They bring mail from friends and family. They make sure people's mail goes to the right places.

Hands On: Be a Stamp Saver

Start a stamp collection. A collection is a group of things gathered over time. You can add to your collection your whole life.

What You Need
- Used stamps
- Warm water
- Paper towels
- A notebook
- A small container
- Tweezers
- A heavy book
- Paste or tape

What You Do
1. Ask friends and family to save their used stamps for you. Remove any paper sticking to the stamps.
2. To do this, place a stamp in warm water. Wait five minutes. The stamp should come off the piece of the paper. Wait a few more minutes if it does not.
3. Use tweezers to remove the stamp from the water.
4. Place the stamp between two paper towels. Place a heavy book on top of the paper towels. Leave it there for 12 to 24 hours.
5. Put your stamps in order. This can be done by their prices. This can also be done by their patterns. Then paste or tape your stamps in a notebook.
6. Look for new and different stamps to save.

Words To Know

mail clerk (MAYL KLURK)—a person who helps mail carriers and other people with the mail
post office (POHST OF-iss)—a building where mail is sorted and stamps are sold
pouch (POUCH)—a bag with a flap over the top
route (ROOT)—the places a mail carrier must go to bring the mail

Read More

Gibbons, Gail. *The Post Office Book: Mail and How It Moves*. New York: Thomas Y. Crowell, 1982.

Marshak, Samuel. *Hail to Mail*. New York: Henry Holt & Company, 1990.

Skurzynski, Gloria. *Here Comes the Mail*. New York: Bradbury Press, 1992.

Internet Sites

United States Postal Service

http://www.usps.gov

Chinese Post Office

http://205.158.7.130/ccc_top/card/card.htm

Index